Watermark

stories from the darker side of love

G.P. Taylor

Watermark

stories from the darker side of love

G.P. Taylor

FBS

Fabulous BookS

www.fbs-publishing.co.uk

First Published in the UK November 2016 by FBS Publishing Ltd.
22 Dereham Road, Thetford,
Norfolk. IP25 6ER

ISBN 978-0-9932043-4-0

Cover design by Owen Claxton
Text Edited by Alasdair McKenzie
Typesetting by Scott Burditt

If I could write a haiku
for the tears
I have cried
It would soon
become a sonnet
for a love
that died.

Darker Side of Love

Words are oft like coffin nails
found in Christmas pudding
no silver coin just
cold comfort for those who sing
the chorus to the darker side of love.
There is no black star and no difference
nothing to look back on in fear or anger
just a dagger of choked arrogance.

It is strange how love can so quickly be forgot.
A marriage thrown away in a dumpster of the mind.
Conversations now unkind,
we soon disregard, that we once were one
held together by God and love.

Then life -

Hacks away as day by day with no reproach
we slowly allow its death.
At first it sluggishly slips
and we forget the joy of each other's lips.

Our words become mercury quick
to pick and tease anger into each phrase
and weeks where we were happy,
now waste away
as if they are diseased, without a cure
and just as Lazarus they will die.

Like the flaked crumbs of tinned chicken pie
we live with second best.
Make do and mend until the end.
Nearly but not quite.
Out of mind, out of sight.
We are
no longer the apple of the eye,
neither loves delight—and
as if love is a bus to Hull
taken by pound shop pilgrims
who are forever disappointed
with their imperfect purchases
our love will never be the same again.

Like a Fool

Fat men in robes said you were good
that all your works were true and bold
and I believed their every word
and behold … they lied.

They spewed the Psalms and Song of Songs
as if a spell to appease the throng
of Angels, saints and sinners
greedily eating bread and wine
like cheap school dinners.

The misguided divine
did not mind the inconsistencies of creed
a god of war and love combined
who kills the meek and makes the innocent bleed.

Purple-clad Pharisees with fat cat salaries,
swindle with words at every turn
to protect the cash of the family firm.
Robbing from the pews with promises
of jam tomorrow, hope and glory

whilst the King of the Jews
looks down from his cross
nailed there by our misery and loss
in this ancient fairy story.

And like a fool I believed
never questioning truths of heaven and hell
with all the world to tell—I too set forth
on the Jesus Jihad
into the land of black and white
where they were wrong and only I was right.
I turned the other cheek
to ignore the weak.
As with burning brimstone hands
I cupped the doubtful sands that
trickled through my conscience-troubled fingers.

Then it came.
The God who loved me as a son,
smote my child
with sickness that no man could take.
So vile—her body wracked with pain and boiling blood
I prayed you would take me—not her—if you could.

And as she laid wired and dying
I cursed your name for lying
you did not heal or save but
only promised riches and redemption in the grave.

In the darkness of that soulless night
when all was lost.
As I waited for her breath to end
and she to be no more.
With open eyes she woke
and your Name said,
as if you stood beside me
silent … invisible … by her door.
When in grief's blackness
I had lost you from my sight.
In her terror you had been
the only Light.

Autocorrect

In a darkened room
with an even darker heart
holding the tablet in his fingers
eyes bright with its glow
he looked at her picture.

A wedding day snapped
by a passing guest
of a beautiful bride
and her beau.
A thin man, narrow chest
dressed in a straw hat
striped blazer and frogman flippers.

Are you happy?

The words were typed easily.
Empty of innocence.
Mischief filled.
They vanished into the messenger
and sped the miles

as if a hungry wolf
in pursuit of this,
his Red Riding Hood.

Perhaps if they had met face to face
he would never have dared.
Perhaps if they had not spoken
he would never have erred.

Remote and distant
his face hidden
she could not glean any feeling
see his eyes devour her
see his bleak intent
on the dark side of the Internet

NO.

The word was alone on the screen
It was all he needed.
And was greeted with a smile
And quickened breath.

Coffin?

He quickly mistyped.
The hasty word sent without autocorrect
a line was already crossed.
In his heart he had decided
to run the prey to ground
and woo her with warm words.

He heard the laughter in her fingers

COFFEE? WHERE? XX

The Watermark

My downfall was delivered
by the bald man
with child and pram
to the Watermark.

With a reluctant smile
He shook my hand
and wiped the perspiration
from his brow.

I offered my seat
but replete, he moaned of boats
summertime yachts,
and how time flies.

In his eyes was rooted doubt
like that in dogs when
in the street they meet
a ragged winter fox.

An hour? He asked her
and with a frown agreed
to leave his bride and child
at the table by the window with me.

Hidden

S kin of porcelain
stretched over bone.
As if the Lady of Shallot,
she turned a ringlet of the reddest hair
wrapped it around her finger
and sighed.

The man stepped closer, older than he cared,
more scared than she would ever understand.
With desire often thought
never to be more than half-hearted reverie
he touched her hand
and banished his fear.

She softly breathed
warm and enfolding—bold.
A smile slipped to her lips as he tiptoed
with banal conversation
about the state of the nation, the price of bread
and a question he thought she would dread

Kiss me?
The words were muttered slowly
and with a drop of the head
her answer was unspoken, a broken look,
face turned to the floor
he pressed her against the door and pulled her close.

Fingers quickly entwined
as if the tongues of snakes
as lips touched that deepest place
his soul was barren of grace
and slipping to hell
the man dare not tell
of love that had simmered
for several summers
Hidden.

The Bride

I'm fine and very lucky to have what I have
(The bride said ... in words ... that were broken and
dead)

There is much I need and he's kind to me too
Though the love we once had died long ago

I am not cared for or wanted
cherished ... but downtrodden
the day we were married in a year was forgotten

It was drowned in the storm at the harbour of bones
And his words were eye candy that nobody owns

I am lost, unrequited, in the mountains of paper
in his meetings, agendas and internet data

I stay through fear
of the judgment of friends
and the gossip of strangers that will never end

I desire my freedom to be who I am
but am frightened of hurting
the man and his lamb

I shall stay for a season in
misery and woe
and always regret that I did not go

for richer and poorer
in sickness and health
all of this
is control by stealth

I will stand on his arm
and smile in right places
at Roundtable, the Masons, Tory candidate races

A trophy bride with ringlets and tears
lost in the good life
of muesli and beer

He comes home late
leaves the dishes until morning

I wake and work
his harsh words scorning

Condemned by faint praise
of

'Oh yes dear that's nice ...'

This is what they call the marital price?

He said

Perhaps you could work in a charity store
but a writer?
a poet?
a laureate?
no more ...

In my eyes
you are just flesh
in a dress.
And your foolish ambitions
will cause you distress

Be Obedient.
Loyal.
Trustworthy.
True.
These bridal words my dear wife,
I speak to you ...

Skin Deep

There are words in life
that stick like twigs
and choke emotion
deep within.

'Goodbye. I am sorry. We have to end.'
Are spoken as if unwelcome guests
to friends and lovers
who stare teary-eyed.
As consonants bite like wolves
with jagged adverb teeth
and bloodstained nouns

The signs are bold
(With the gift of hindsight)
but often ignored
in the here and now
when love dies.

It could never be? Who? me?

Words that were once warm grow cold.
Arms that once hugged
are no longer bold.
Sighing eyes now look away.
And once loved conversations are mostly ignored
as night ends day.

'We cannot go on.'
Are words thought often
but often too afraid to say
like a crow-dark day.
With sleepless hours
and counting clocks
in running dreams
of the girl in a fairy frock.

And what from this life do we ever learn?
that love is fickle
and words are cheap
and beauty is never more than
skin deep.

So Did a Dragon?

So did a dragon lock you there?
And snip away each strand of hair
With cutting words that broke your heart
To tear your soul wide apart

So did a dragon make a key?
From the heartache of your misery
Did suspicious ropes catch the child?
That wandered in the world so wild

So did a dragon nail the door?
With anger at the tears it saw
And all the things you never said
That kept the monster from your bed

So did a dragon build a house?
To keep you as his domestic mouse
Your parlour now a prison be
To keep true love away from thee.

Into the Woods

Hand in hand and step by step
in silence they walk the sunlit bracken path
until the canopy of evergreens
stifles their breath with pine scent.

Day is made dark by thick branches
and upon the needle carpet
a blanket of tartan is cast,
amongst the deathbed stillness.

This is their secret place where
names are carved upon the tree
and bound together with a rope cartouche
as if for all eternity.

No Bible black code of life
is in this place,
no disgrace for the pleasure
of another man's wife.

Into the woods
they take their love
in hope they can escape the godly eye
that judges them from above.

Here they can hear no wagging tongues
that gossip where the wood ends
and chant their names like wayward sisters,
as if to break the spell and make amends.

They kiss and moments pass
two entwine and give their all
naked but not corrupt,
as a sorrowful magpie calls.

And resting, spent, still deep within,
breath mingling with breath
they talk in whispers and hope
their love will only end with death.

The Beekeeper

In the company of bees, she walks through life
amongst mottled clouds of wings and stings with
her eyes cast down
in shrouds of heather pollen that falls through sun
fingers as if solstice dust.

On a lace-gloved hand the bitter twist, barbed and strong
punctures deep and true, as poison pumps a venom mist
and the Beekeeper smiles—this is her life—a metaphor
for all her pain and heartbreak is more than this.

Here is honesty of revenge, no malice aforethought of
the Bee
no bitterness or jealousy or anger does she see.
As Hell empties itself of devils into her hand,
like Sycorax she stands and waits to watch it fly away
gutted, disembowelled without its lance.

No more to dance in hives and pathways give, it dies.
The Beekeeper takes the netted shroud from her head
and hopes that all her woes would too be dead.

Umbilicus

Before dawn
crept through window slats,
like the tongue of a snake
his finger slid down my neck
and to my breast.

That which had once fed his child
was clumsily twisted
between thumb and finger.
His hand did not linger as
I tried to hold
your face in my mind.

His touch was unkind
like harsh words
as his desire I denied
until inside he knifed,
cutting through my reluctant flesh,
forcing the purse's clasp.

There was no gasp of joy
as feigning sleep
I gave no moans of love
As with tight lips whispered your name.

He shuddered and withdrew
showering my body with his dew
and without compassion
rolled from me
leaving a pool of his contempt
in the cup of my umbilicus.

Godot

He waits like a child for Christmas
and in growing anticipation,
sees that day
slip further away.

Asking for a time and a place,
the month's race ahead
into the distance.
Over the horizon
like a sailing ship
blown by October gales.

He promised he would wait
as if for Godot
and sing a recursive round
of death's despair for a dog
a vague supplication
for whom he cared.
But now, he sees that vow
slipping through his fingers.

Each day impatience
like impertinent thoughts
makes him wonder
how long can he wait?
Until hell is bound by ice?
And age and decay
are all that his feeble eyes can see?

'I will wait for you …
just as long as it takes …'
are idle words that slip quickly
from the jealous tongue
and when begun
become like bindings
that hold him fast
to his forlorn oath.

He waits
resigned to the fate
that she might never come
and like Vladimir and Estragon
who sit on stones
under Irish trees
may never meet his friend.
He gives his heart
and even though she swears
undying love, knows
they will always be apart.

The Mouse and the Toad

Just a matter of time said the mouse
and then the trap snapped
snicker snack, the bar fell
a death knell, clicked and crashed
muesli spilled, over frilled frocks
and mortise locks.

In the house
the mouse, mort-blue like woad
did not want to kiss the toad
who sparked and barked
with angry words
and offered arguments absurd
of why and how and who and where
but in his heart there was no care.

His life had been a fancy dress
of frogman flippers and quiet distress
of wedding hats and stuffed fat cats
that stared at taxidermy crows
with broken beaks and pantyhose.

He questioned mouse about her life
And why she had become his wife
The fairy child that sealed the knot
on the day that he forgot.

Toad searched the house for her mistake
when a Fox she did take
into the woods and under the trees
whilst Toad was left to tend his bees.

And in the forest the fox and mouse
Conversed on where to build their house
Sipping from bone cups tenderly
Fox took the mouse upon his knee
'Good Mouse, Good Mouse,'
he whispered sweet
'Was it through fate that we did meet?'
'Dear Fox, Dear Fox,'
the mouse replied
'Do you want *me* to be *your* bride?'

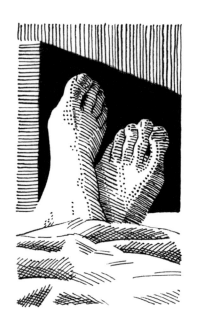

Green Silk

On green silk, she takes his head
under the bronze chandelier
of a fine seaside terrace with magnolia walls
then holds him in long fingers
as on the bed kisses the meatus lip
and sips the silver milt
that spills from the tip.

No prisoner is he, though he be bound
in tethers of love and leather
like a mistletoe pig being led to slaughter
a Christmas fancy wrapped in gaudy yarn.
Then as one dying he holds fast to life
with hands like a village blacksmith,
gulping every breath as juddering death
overcomes him with evermore delight.

The woman laughs as she wipes her hand across his chest
and taking the hem of his vest mops her mouth.
No words are said or needed on this bed.
Here they lie each Wednesday

to stare at ceiling cracks
as if branches of a spreading chestnut tree,
and as they talk of life, though she, (not his wife)
holds him tenderly.

Domestic Guernica

Behind the painted door
in the hallway, plain and suburban,
iron fists and steel brow
beat and punch
with motiveless malignancy.

On the ordinary stairs
the small girl cries.
As in his anger the brute lies
like unequals they clash
whilst punches smash.

The boy sighs—blackened eyes
beaten by the man,
a husband with tight hands
laminated with the demands
of contempt for his wife
to bruise with distrust and strife
ingrained in each finger
that slapped his child back and forth
and no force could stop.

A punishment for what he had done
given with a promise that he would
do much more.

And yet,
nothing could wash the fear
from the eyes of the child.
She and only she
will carry that misery
through the tears of her life
wondering why the wife
could not
would not
did not stop
the Guernica blows
that beat and beat as under feet
the boy was kicked and trashed
and pushed from the house
as the man in his arrogance
holds tight
to his silent domestic mouse.

Guests

In my head are unwelcome guests.
Men in drag who shout and scream
and nag like washer women
gossiping over Council hedges
whilst washing windows, steps and ledges
in rolled-down stockings and slipper-covered feet
as like sheep in wolf coats they bicker and bleat.

In my head are unwelcome guests.
Ladies in frocks who haul me
back and forth in ebb and swells
drowning in waves and torrents
up mountains and through dark dells
of happiness and loathing
casting spells like witches on the heath.

In my head are unwelcome guests.
Children in shrouds with sallow faces
screaming and crying like Belsen brides
as in their misery cannot decide
between life and death
as with typhus breath they gasp their last
and sing goodbye to life in pinstriped socks.

Good Friday

He is alone on the bed
mind racing, not sleeping
Prayers unanswered
as nothing is said.
Reaching out in darkness
he twists imagined hair
between his fingers as
his memory lingers.
On the scent of myrrh
red wine and silver cup
crumbed bread, stone tablets
to the dead.
The room is his Church
dark and alone
he keeps watch
a memory of former things
and the scent of gin.
He speaks—
the words echo
as they spill from his lips
and wonders if sin

deafened his imaginary friend.
The one he worshipped
stood in his shrine
gave sacrifice in mourning
memorial.
He looks to the wall as dawn breaks
streetlights cast a shadow
old and rugged.
A Friday reminder of one man
taken, beaten, bones crushed, nailed to wood.
He asks himself
did it do the world any good?
The catechism of guilt became the shank
to stab his heart.
Then he sleeps
unable to watch another hour
and like that other Peter,
his life
betrays his master.
As the cock crows.

The Bridge

On Valley Road
A broad bridge stands
with four stone spears
that pierce the ground
A viaduct for the ways of men
And upon its road
many lives tread
and many end.

Drawn to their death
Without judgement or grace
They chose this arch of grit and steel
To be their final resting place.
Each in distress
climbed the wire wall
and all alone
they fall.

And now.

Copper green bars like baboon teeth
hold back a penitential man
caged in this life.
He scrambles up the wires
and on the mesh canopy.
Far out to sea
seagulls call and waves roar,
the sinner on the bridge demands no more.

As in his head voices scream
of love and lives
that are intertwined like
the steel net on which he clings.
With knuckled hands frightened to let go
he smiles.

As leaves in autumn fall
wearisome of their
connection to the tree
So does he.

Without scream or sigh
he flies momentarily

and Mother Earth
accelerates her grasp
reaches out
pulls him to her concrete womb
crushing sinew and bone
as his blood stains the road.

Who was this man
who sacrificed himself?
As the voices raged
inside his head
and offered him the comfort
of the sleeping grateful dead.

What force of man or solitude
brought him to this place?
Where in disgrace his family
now stand
with funeral gifts
of flowers and photographs
as with trembling hands
they build a shrine.

I Fooled Myself

I fooled myself with immortal thoughts,
that in my human frailty
could make myself Methuselah.

No forethought was ever given to death,
or loss or grief or where and when
would be that final breath.

And then it came upon my bed—
a January cough of spittle blood,
at first of little consequence.

With Curie's light it was exposed,
beating weakly, failing heart.
Gnarled, twisted, failing, old.

I often thought that
life would end in great old age
on a fog filled February afternoon.

Now all had changed
In several words of medically
confirmed deliberation—I had a date.

Within three years and no more than seven
G-d would call me home
And give me proof of heaven.

GHOSTS

On a Singapore Beach - 1942

You were my last thought on a Singapore beach
Sun filled my eyes and the surf whispered on
warm sand
I was bold and did not cry like some other men
as one by one they gave up this world.
But then, unlike they, I had a memory of your face
And not one trace of sadness filled my heart.
For to depart life I had no fear.
It was your lips I remembered most
Soft and moist, coated in the last of your lipstick
Rationed, you dipped your finger in the final drop.
Before I could recall your kiss, the sword fell
old cold steel of hate did seal my fate.
Now I find there is no death, no final breath or sigh
Life leads to life and no love's labour is ever lost.

The Lawn Mower

In the spare room
of a Regency house
standing by the window
Mrs. Abernathy
looks out over fogged lawns.

For her part
her dim and feeble heart
had memory of a long ago death.
A deceit of the mind
thoughts deemed too unkind to speak.

Twisting the hessian curtains
with long bone fingers
she lingers on the remembrance
and wonders
if it belongs to another.

Perhaps the spectre who walks the hall
with night time footsteps
that with tip—tap—tip—tap
disturbs her sleep

The wanderer whom she seldom sees
but hears the aghast ghost
in a Tootal scarf
that one night was glimpsed singing Christmas songs
with charming nouns and loving verbs

Watching the last leaves fall from dying elms
she waits for
his sometime appearance
pushing a trolley with small iron wheels
and spinning blades that eat the grass.

In the late evening
as she was grieving her earthly loss
he smoked a pipe under the araucana
and rapping in protest on the window glass
she was ignored.

Three Times Three

Each morning by the kitchen door I find
a ring of stones placed neatly
in a mosaic of a rose.
Always stolen are the silver spoons
emptied from the rack
a repose, hidden in bleak exchange
never to be given back.
On the window glass are clumsy marks
as if the daubing of a child
with butter-smudged fingers.
Like the sound of skylarks
from high in the house a girl recites
three times three—is nine,
four times three—is twelve.
Her footsteps rattle the shelves
as she skips along the bedroom floor
and then stops
her game in time she has forgot.
Though I not her mother be
she calls my name.
I answer in soft whispers tenderly,

frightened that she might reply.
On the stairs her footsteps
wane and die in faintness without vanity
and staring in the hallway looking glass
I see a small and fading child.
With half a smile in dim reflection
she looks me in the eye.
As all around her mouth the pox I see,
again she says my name ... *Emily.*

Mrs. Abernathy

In the spare room
of my Regency house
I see her face,
sometimes glimpsed in window glass
as long shadows
are cast by the araucana tree.

I smoke a pipe and there she stands
looking down on me.
Thin-faced,
white hair,
a countenance of grace.

When I glance up
she smiles and then is gone
but once tapped on the window
as I mowed the lawn
and in the spinning blades
killed a September frog.

The parson said
this ghost means no harm
and would not pray
for her to be gone
to rest in peace, deceased from this life.

No bell, book and candle
could he give.
Just mutterings of her perfect life
and how in much widowed strife
she would manicure
the flowers around the choir.

She built the church
and gave a spire
casting a low bell
in her husband's name
and without shame
sent the poor to school.

This was Mrs. Abernathy,
still tied to this world
and taken from it
by slight of hand and accident
of a half-chewed chicken bone.

It was her rasped and consumptive cough
that I heard at first,
as the garden cleared of October fog
and later as I ate poached eggs
her words begged for me to come.

She called me from the upper hall
distinctive, shrill without a name.
I came and stood at the foot of the stairs
and heard her dreaded tread
tip—tap—tip—tap.

Every day when I am alone
I listen to her whisper on the stairs
she cries her cares and reverie
in the morning room
at half past three.

At Christmas as we gathered around the fire
her voice echoed in the gallery
accompanying our bawdy choir
as we stood around the tree
my wife, my child and me
heard her softly sing.

Like this blithe spirit I will never leave this place.
Even when late at night I met
Mrs. Abernathy face to face.
She shouted and cajoled
and tried to cast me out, quite bold
as if I were the ghost not she.

Then frightened she ran,
screaming to an upper room
where in darkness and gloom she stomped her feet
like a recalcitrant child
as doors slammed back and forth
and her words were constant and muttered in wrath.

Too much for my wife and child
in this place of blood-red brick upon brick
slate upon slate, stone upon stone,
was left to my fate, alone, as I, unwilling to leave
or give up my house to a ghost.
stayed all these years.

Without fear, I walk the corridors
empty and long and listen
for a solstice song,
and perhaps this is my hell
I the ghost
and she, Mrs. Abernathy, alive and well?

The Girl with a Tiger's Heart

In the darkest forest of a desolate mind
is a girl with a tiger's heart
she roams each thought
in a vintage dress
to rip your love apart.

In the darkest forest of a desolate mind
is a girl with a tiger's eyes
she hunts you down
to drink your blood
with desire that never dies.

In the darkest forest of a desolate mind
is a girl with a tiger's claws
she summons you
in silk and lace
and dances to your faint applause.

In the darkest forest of a desolate mind
is a girl with a tiger's dread
through sleepless nights
she stalks your soul
to devour you in your bed.

The Girl with String on her Fingers

Momma's kind words can't keep me here
there is a world outside this place
if only I can remember where
and how and what she said
to her little girl with auburn hair
caught in life's dreary chase
and forgetful shame's disgrace.

'You gotta remember what Momma says,'
words dreamed away in echoes already fled
as the bus doors shut and the driver yells
and Momma waves and tries to tell
her little girl of love to the moon and back
that she will remember on dark days
when Momma is dead.

'I'll tie string on your fingers then you'll know.'
Blue for school, green for shops and red?
If only I could recall all the things she said
as we stood by the gate
I in my marigold dress
and she, with all her love, holds me
closer than I have ever been held again.

'Blue string for shop and green for school,'
words said as she wipes away tears with soft fingers
and her smile strips all she says from my mind
bright sun and long days tainted with the scent
of elderflowers, and cut grass cannot take away
the memory of her face and finger string that did not
last
in a remembered place of times past.

And red ... how now I can recall
her words
and red ... because ...

HIDING PLACES

Monday Morning in a Cumbrian Town

Grey slates,
wet like dragon scales
rest on dark stones
windowed and doored.

A nowhere town
of fat women in thick tights
with delinquent brats
that dangle from their fingers
like broken street lamps.

They trip, tramp
to the market place
where a Fleetwood fish seller
offers them hake
from the back of a van
where every Monday he stands
as cold rain washes cod skin
from his nicotine-stained fingers.

The kids bleat
as they are dragged through
damp streets
weather-washed with
autumn's first flood.

The sentinel tick tocks
and chimes the hours
a fine town clock
etched with names of the noble dead
that only on one day in November are read.

Ignored with eyes of those who pass by are
Burrell
Brockbank
Hulse
Platt.

Lives no longer remembered
in the morning
as the shop keeper wipes the bloodied knife
on his butcher's apron
having sliced a steak

of salt marsh lamb
grown and grazed on the grave
where the slave boy sleeps.

And on Faraday Road
they trudge to school
aged teachers with lessons learnt
who dream of making geniuses out of fools
and building cathedrals
from broken bricks.

Cyclist speed by
old men in skintight Lycra
panting on pedal irons
of gossamer carbon
sprinting out of town towards
the barricade of Pennine hills.

And still, as the town wakes
one by one cardigan-clad shop assistants
open doors towards the empty town.
And the road leads in and the road leads out
But no one stops.

On Lakeland Roads

Beside the lake, beneath the trees
they walk with Wainwright
to the grave of a poet long dead
with sonnets half remembered
and his words now unread.

Wrapped in Gore-tex
to protect them from the chill
of their iced cappuccino.
Bought from shops
geared to sell
their waterproof, breathable
outdoor shell.

They wander lonely in the crowd
of Japanese tourists clutching
Beatrix at her best.
With Peter Rabbit,
and Mr. Tod
they snip snap and Polaroid
every moment.

At odds with themselves.
They walk in boots
made for mountains
they will never climb.
As if to tell drinkers
at Ambleside cafés
of a hope or maybe
a future fell conquest.

A uniform
that is worn
by all who come here.
Rucksack
Gaiters
Bottle
Map

Now packed in pubs
with Gastro grub
they smugly snuggle
in a North Face fleece
keys in pocket
to a second home
outwaged and outpriced
to the man behind the bar.

He serves and smiles
and walks the miles
from The Mason's Arms
on Lakeland roads
lined with houses owned
by incomers.

To be read out loud …

L ife …
        Got to get it right.
        No second chance to
change the dance
this ain't no rehearsal
it's this then a funeral

Got to be amazing.
Stargazing
to conquer the earth in
every verse.
No shit bits.
or bitchin' fits.
Each word spoken
isn't just a token

Got to get it right.
Got to be amazing.
No use crazing
about mistakes
or the cost of cupcakes

Got to make them right.
Escape to the night
looking for the light.
Got to get it right.
walk out the door
find a new dance floor.

Epilogue

Watermark is a collection of writing from the heart. I try not to polish the pieces of work and allow them to rest on the page as they have been written. The words are usually birthed as I drive or walk and dictated into my iPhone. I then use Dragon software to get them on to the page as text. Little is then done to the words. They are not laboured over or greatly edited but allowed to be just what they are, quickly spoken, brief images of imagination.

It is my desire that you hear them as I have spoken them—they convey raw thoughts, ideas and emotions. For me, poetry is sharing the life and sentiments of the writer. It is a window into their lives, small stories they want to tell.

This short collection chronicles a period of my life where I had been suffering from ill health and a treasured relationship ended and another began. It was a time when I struggled with my faith and tried to uncover who I really was and not what life had made me.

Enjoy.
G.P. Taylor. December 2015

About the Author

G.P. Taylor is a *New York Times*, award-winning bestselling writer. He has written over twenty books for children and adults. His work is translated into over fifty languages.

http://www.gptaylor.info

www.fbs-publishing.co.uk